Towards the Dawn

Mary Hathaway
Illustrations by John Haysom

A LION BOOK
Tring · Batavia · Sydney

Published by
Lion Publishing plc
Icknield Way, Tring, Herts, England
ISBN 0 7459 1116 1
Albatross Books Pty Ltd
PO Box 320, Sutherland, NSW 2232, Australia
ISBN 0 86760 808 0

First edition 1987

Acknowledgments
Bible quotations from *Good News Bible,*
copyright © 1966, 1971 and 1976 American
Bible Society, published by Bible Societies/Collins

Printed and bound in Great Britain by
Purnell Book Production Ltd, Paulton, Bristol
Member of the BPCC Group

Introduction

In the space of a year in my early twenties, I underwent surgery for a thyroid complaint, suffered a broken engagement and had a nervous breakdown. It seemed as if I would never lead a normal life again. But eventually, with specialist help, the healing process began.

Knowing from the inside the misery of depression, I have put together some pieces of my own writing and some verses from the Bible which helped me during that time, in the hope that others who suffer may perhaps find in them stepping stones to help them through their own darkness.

For I do believe it is possible to come through. Although I still get depressed at times, I can see that one of the verses from the Bible I found very precious is beginning to come true for me.

'The winter is over,
the rains have stopped;
in the countryside
the flowers are in bloom,
this is the time for singing.'

Mary Hathaway

Let the Storm Break

Let the storm break.
Don't push it to the back of your mind
or pretend it isn't there.
Storms that are hidden
become savage things.
It is better to let the storm come and weep
than to let it stay hidden
and turn the heart sour and bitter.
Tears are a cleansing stream.

Let the storm break –
all the pent up sorrow, pain and despair –
bow your head and let it flow over you.
And then, though your spirit feels crushed
and utterly broken,
after a little while the impossible will happen
and you will raise your head again.
Life will creep back into your numbed spirit.
But, best of all,
the storm will have blown itself out
and once again your whole being will be free,
free and cleansed and able to love.

*Lord, you have examined me
and you know me.
You know everything I do;
from far away you understand
all my thoughts.
You see me, whether I am working or resting;
you know all my actions.
Even before I speak,
you already know what I will say.
You are all round me on every side;
you protect me with your power.
Your knowledge of me is too deep;
it is beyond my understanding.*

From Psalm 139, verses 1-6

Two Pierced Hands

I had a sorrow so deep
that human love could not penetrate
its deepest recesses.
I stumbled through the valley
of suffering in my mind,
down, down into the depths of the darkness.
And there in the tearless pain beyond pain
I saw two hands outstretched.
Two pierced hands —
that was all I could see —
two pierced hands held out to me.

I knew that my sorrow was shared
to the uttermost,
that I did not stand alone in the darkness,
that every part of my pain was understood.
Two loving hands —
that was all I could see —
two loving hands held out to me.

I felt no lessening of pain.
The stark reality of sorrow was still there,
to be faced and lived with.
But I was not alone.
In healing silence
two pierced hands had held mine
in the depths of that darkness.
Two sharing hands –
that was all I had seen –
two sharing hands held out to me.

CIRCLE OF THORNS

God of the storm and rain,
God of the wild sea raging,
hear me, hear my crying.
God of the uncontrollable,
God of the mind of man,
hear me, hear my crying.
God of the circle of thorns,
God dead and living again,
bring me through this dying
to find you real again.

God of the circle of thorns,
hear me — in your mercy.

Candle at Dusk

As darkness falls,
so your flame
grows ever brighter.
The night crowds in,
shadows rushing down
on every side –
but they do not put you out.
And the flame that seemed
so small, so insignificant
against the sun,
comes into its own
with the deepening of the night.

As a hen shelters
her chickens under her wings
from danger,
so the newborn shadows
of the gathering dusk
fly to you –
darkness sheltering
under the wings
of light.

So burn in me
candle of God.

Let your love
draw all my shadows
swiftly to yourself.
So when night comes
and fears and doubts
and every kind of sin
bear down upon my spirit,
let me bring them
to your light knowing
that it shines best
against the blackest darkness.

As a hen shelters
her chickens under her wings
from danger,
so I fly to you
that I may dwell in safety —

for in my darkness
I also need the shelter
of your wings
of light.

*Be merciful to me, O God, be merciful,
because I come to you for safety.
In the shadow of your wings I find protection
until the raging storms are over.*

From Psalm 57, verse 1

*Trust in the Lord with all your heart.
Never rely on what you think you know.
Remember the Lord in everything you do,
and he will show you the right way.*

Proverbs 3, verses 5-6

So I Shall Feel the Waves

'When you go through deep waters
and great trouble,
I will be with you.
When you go through rivers
of difficulty,
you will not drown.
When you walk through the fire
of oppression,
you will not be burned up,
the flames will not consume you.'

Isaiah 43, verse 2

So I shall feel the waves
and hear the storm,
the waters will sometimes cover me,
the currents will pull at my feet,
I shall be afraid for my life,

but –
I shall not drown.

So I shall feel the heat,
I shall be scorched,
I shall be burned,
and despair of my life,

but —
the flames will not consume me.

You do not promise a life
full of frothy joy,
you promise *life* —
in all its fullness,
with its pain and suffering
as well as its love and joy.

You are real, Lord,
you are true, Lord,
and I rest in your word
in my despair and confusion
in the sure knowledge
that I *shall* come through.

Fragment

This is not the finish of the song,
only a pause in the singing.
I do not know the music,
that is all.

This is not the ending of the way,
only the beginning.
I do not know where to go,
that is all.

How this desert can become
a watered garden,
I do not know,
that is all —

but God is still God.

FEAR

This morning I saw someone else afraid
and I was sad to see so much fear.
For I know fear well –
he has been my constant companion.
Fear is more terrible than pain.

It is good not to be afraid.
But to know fear
and go back and conquer it
is a greater victory.
For all mankind knows fear
and lives with it
but few break out of its prison.

To conquer fear
is to step out into sunlight
from the shadow.
It is to have the freedom of the skies
after living in a cage.
It is to look life in the face,
the past, the present and the future
and to know they are but servants,
not domineering masters,
enslaving, crippling,
stunting every good potential.

So Lord, in your mercy,
help me win this battle
because no one could have been
more afraid than I.
That is why it is imperative
that I should win –

so Lord, in your mercy,
help me to win!

Come to me, all of you who are tired
from carrying heavy loads,
and I will give you rest.
Take my yoke and put it on you,
and learn from me,
because I am gentle and humble in spirit,
and you will find rest.

From Matthew's Gospel, chapter 11, verses 28-30

Made Anew with Love

I have watched
the ruin of my life
and seen no hope
of resurrection.

Yet I know
I too shall live
and see a purpose
in my pain
and harvest light
out of my darkness.
For I shall stand,
not broken down and desolate
before my God,
but tall and beautiful
and made anew with love.